I0436236

Psycho-linguistics, Cognition, and Issues

Thomas Hodge

Table of Contents

Anterograde Amnesia

The concept of losing one's memories is highly related to cognitive psychology in that memories determine how one perceives the world, and a lack of prior information affects the way in which one processes new information. Without the ability to create new memories, communicating with others and trusting the environment poses new challenges. Existing schemas of knowledge would have to be continually rebuilt. Advancing through a conversation would involve restarting that conversation repeatedly. Communication would serve to only be temporary, and the individual would need to continually be refreshed concerning prior point in the conversation.

In examining this topic, several psychological terms are referred to concerning anterograde amnesia. First, the concept of declarative memory is an important concept to understand when examining anterograde amnesia. This is the facts that one can clearly recall from memory. Decay theory and interference theory are also two significant psychological concepts when considering anterograde amnesia. These two theories refer to the way in which one forgets information. Decay theory views forgetting in the light that traces of memories simply deteriorate. Interference theory explains that prior traces of memory are simply distorted by newly learned information.

Anterograde amnesia relates to the topic of perception which has been previously discussed in the class very explicitly. Not being able to develop new memories has a profound effect on how one perceives their environment due distrust which would develop from their inability to develop new memories. This inability would also serve to constantly reset the individual's perception of the world to their perception of the world around the time that the condition began. Anterograde amnesia can be viewed as not only an impairment of memory, but it can also be seen as impairment to one's ability to change their perception of the world.

In considering anterograde amnesia patients, the condition would be useful in providing a better understanding of what information is more likely to be retained for longer periods of time. A potential research question would be to ask, "How can information be retained for longer periods of time?" Several studies have been conducted to learn more about the effects of anterograde amnesia on patients. In the research conducted by Dewar, Della Sala, Beschin, and Cowan (2010), evidence was found that interference of newer information had a strong effect on the individuals' difficulties with maintaining information for long periods of time. This provides sight into not only the condition of anterograde amnesia but also how regular people retain and forget information. The research of Diamond and Rozin (1984) found that information that was broken to smaller units could be retained for much longer periods of time. This type of insight into how memories are retained serves to show that several factors regarding how the information is learned and stored affect how well it is retained.

In popular culture, amnesia is sometimes seen as a tool that can be used to clear out the memories of an individual like in the movie *Paycheck* (Chang, Davis, Hacket, & Woo, 2003). Popular fiction has utilized research on anterograde amnesia in the case of *Paycheck* (Chang et al., 2003) to erase the main characters memories for the purpose of protecting sensitive information. This use of anterograde amnesia research shows how such research can be used to protect information from being revealed because the individual would no longer remember the secrets to divulge the information to others. The uses that popular fiction sees for amnesia research serve to advance the deletion of memories as opposed to current research that is aimed at improving memory efficacy. The text book and current research view anterograde amnesia as an obstacle to be overcome while popular fiction has turned it into a tool to be used for the advancement of self-interested individuals.

There are several implications for the research involved with anterograde amnesia. The research could be used to improve teaching techniques in school so that the information could be presented in a way that would allow it to be better retained. The research could allow for sensitive information to be deleted from one's memory as can be seen in *Paycheck* (Chang et. al., 2003). More optimistically, the research could be seen a positive step into fully understanding how memories are preserved in the mind of an individual over periods of time. If the breaks that occur in anterograde amnesia patients are discovered, these links could be corrected in the patients and also strengthened in regular individuals to improve the memory capacity of average people and improve the quality of their lives.

In conclusion, anterograde amnesia serves as a unique condition that prevents individuals from making new long-term memories. Through research on the topic, many of the details about how memories are stored and translated in the mind can be unlocked. Popular fiction holds a more pessimistic view on research into anterograde amnesia. Popular fiction sees the research to be used to further the self-interest of corporations and powerful individuals. In comparison to current research, popular fiction is considerably more pessimistic. Research into the effects of amnesia truly does show potential for future improvements.

Artificial Intelligence

The concept of artificial intelligence is profoundly related to the study of cognitive psychology. Cognition can be seen as the study of how knowledge is acquired and processed. For a man-made creation to be intelligent, this entity would need to be capable of cognition. Research into artificial intelligence and into cognitive psychology aid each other in improving the understanding how the mind functions. If one could create an artificial intelligence, this artificial intelligence could aid cognitive researchers in better understanding how cognitive functions occur. Cognitive research aids the developers of artificial intelligence in creating machines that learn tasks and improve performance through cognitive concepts.

In the study of artificial intelligence, numerous psychological terms have been used to describe the processes or lack of processes that occur in the man-made devices that have been created to mimic intelligent behavior. The processes typically are examined in terms of their information processing abilities. In the film *Transcendent Man* (Ptolemy & Ptolemy 2008), many of the individuals examine and explain devices capable of processing information and simulating learning from a behaviorist perspective. The artificial intelligence is simply processing inputs (stimuli) and organizing the information into functional outputs (responses) based on pre-designated instructions.

In regards to specific topics in cognitive psychology, artificial intelligence clearly relates with the study of cognitive neuroscience. As cognitive neuroscience is concerned with biological reactions that occur in relation to the brain and other elements of the nervous system, the study of artificial intelligence is concerned with designing a similar system to the human nervous system. The artificial intelligence would be capable of developing improved patterns of logic independent of outside manipulation. Computer chips have been serving to function as the neurons of these devices that simulate intelligent though. The methods of information storage by neurons clearly can be seen as related to the designs of the computer chips that have been advancing the developments in artificial intelligence technology.

Developments in artificial intelligence could lead to technological advances in various fields that would improve the quality of life for humanity. The medical uses of intelligent nano-devices could produce mechanical versions of antibiotics that could neutralize pathogens in the body. To do this, the nano-devices would need to be able to make distinctions concerning very minor differences in organisms. Similarly, nanotechnology could be used to develop devices that repair damaged tissue. For such devices to be effective, a sense of intelligence would need to exist allowing the devices to learn what functions living organism perform and changes that the body would undergo through time. If the devices could determine learn what changes occur, it would then advance its knowledge by gathering new information through observations. Research into artificial intelligence would also allow for an improved understanding of the causes of learning impairments, disabilities, and various mental disorders. By creating working models of how intelligent thought is processed, researchers would be able to narrow down the causes of such impairments. By understanding the causes more clearly, this would allow improved treatments of various disorders and impairments. By knowing how information is processed, one would also be able to improve on the current methods of learning and teaching new information. If one better understands how information is learned and stored, adjustments could be made to the current models of teaching in the education system to increase efficacy in the education system.

Despite the numerous improvements that could be brought about by advances in artificial intelligence, popular culture has taken a pessimistic view of artificial intelligence. This view began as early as 1818 with the classic novel *Frankenstein* (Shelley, 1994). *Frankenstein* created the concern about humans creating other intelligent life. The novel addressed the fear that intelligent beings created by humans would lack the ability to make moral judgments and that the creations would act solely in self-interest. The flaw in the design of an artificial intelligence would be that the being would function as an anti-social entity that would not be capable of determining the difference between right and wrong but only performing actions based on the calculations of whether the results would improve its own well-being. Popular culture has since advanced the basic ideas of Shelley's novel in more recent representations to images of humanity's possible destruction being brought about by intelligent machines like in *Terminator 2: Judgment Day* (1991). In nearly two centuries, popular culture has created a high degree of concern over the consequence of creating intelligent machines that would be more intelligent than humans. The fear is that humanity would become servants to its own creation.

Current research into artificial intelligence shows some positive uses of artificial intelligence. Cleophas and Cleophas (2010) examined a back propagation artificial neural network that utilized methods of learning from examples as opposed to acting upon preset parameters to follow. The program made predictions concerning medical diagnoses utilizing SPSS. The neural network was able to correct itself based on trial and error to improve its results over time. The program did this through a series of algorithms and complex mathematical equations to adjust its predictions based on the correctness or incorrectness of prior predictions. This allowed for the neural network to effectively learn in a sense. Computer programs are ran by a code of that it follows much like how living cells run based off of DNA code. As the program corrected its own code, it evolved to an improved state of performance over a period of time through trial and error. The application of the neural network's learning through negative and positive feedback resulted in improved predictions and diagnoses. By utilizing artificial intelligence in this way to refine medical diagnoses, errors could be more easily avoided in medical practice improving medical treatment for patients experience a wide array of ailments.

In comparing the movie *Transcendent Man*, popular culture, and the current research, one can notice clear differences among the three views of artificial intelligence. Ray Kurzweil holds a highly optimistic view of artificial intelligence applications that are far more radically advanced than current research and technology can support. Some of the artificial intelligence applications he describes for the near future could clearly be supported by current research. In stark contrast, popular culture has a vastly pessimistic view of artificial intelligence as being a danger to individuals and humanity as a whole. Popular culture shows artificial intelligence as being the undoing of humanity and a danger to society as seen in numerous movies and books. Current research is not as advanced currently as either would suggest. Artificial intelligence still abides by the rules of programming codes and has yet to come to the state of self-realization that would be needed in order for an artificial intelligence to decisions based on self-interest. The current research does demonstrate that artificial intelligence can be used to better the quality of life for mankind.

In light of advances in artificial intelligence, neural plasticity would be a topic that could be examined more clearly. As the machine learns new information, adjustments would need to be made to the routing of information across the underlying circuitry that processes information. Examining the changes made to circuitry upon learning in a model that would be similar to the human brain would allow for improved understanding of how the brain is re-wired upon learning. The mathematical patterns could be adapted for the more complex patterns of the human mind after a great deal of research. This would, however provide a base of understanding in how the mind adjusts to accommodate new learning.

Trusting the Numbers

When an individual makes a decision when being provided relevant information, the individual is influenced by several cognitive biases frequently. These biases tend to steer the individual from make the best possible to answer toward one that is not as good. These biases are important to cognitive research due to the fact that they serve as devices that sway the decisions of individual from logical decisions to illogical decisions. As an individual's decisions change from one judgment to another, this affects what will be communicated to others. In examining this matter, several psychological terms are relevant such as the gambler's fallacy, the prescriptive model, and the descriptive model. The prescriptive model involves examining a decision based on statistical analysis, and the descriptive model is the inaccurate method which people actually use in making decisions. The gambler's fallacy is a belief that some individuals have that an event that has not occurred over a long period of time is more likely to occur due to the period of time that has passed without it occurring. In relation to other topics, these biases are relevant because they will affect how an individual develops expertise on a topic and will also present priming opportunities that will interfere with retrieval of pertinent information that corresponds to the decision. If a bias is in place, the bias will inhibit other relevant information from being considered by the individual when making decisions.

Research from Johnson, Tellis, and Macinnis (2005) examined individuals who were buying and selling shares on the stock market. The subjects showed a variation of the gambler's fallacy when examined. As stocks had a trend of doing poorly, the individuals had a tendency to believe that the stocks were due for improvement due to the time since they had last had an improvement. This belief showed gradual decrease over longer periods of time as the stock continued to perform poorly. The effects of the gambler's fallacy increased steadily until a point and then proceeded to decrease as the negative trend continued. Ross and Degroot (1982) found that adolescences were more likely to be swayed by the gambler's fallacy bias when problems built upon each other with higher degrees of similarities than when differences were greater between problems. This study could be perceived as showing how repetition of decisions could lead to the gambler's fallacy. In examining the issue of cognitive biases further, a potential research question could serve as questioning what mental processes promote the occurrence of the gambler's fallacy in individuals. This question would pertain to individual's developing a mental fatigue to the repetition of similar responses.

In contrast to falling victim to the gambler's fallacy, popular fiction examines the possible applications in overcoming this bias and what could happen if one were to make decisions based upon the prescriptive model. This can be clearly seen in *21*(Spacey and Luketic, 2008). In the film, college students are training to examine the statistical possibilities of certain cards being drawn in blackjack games. As the students bet accordingly with the best statistical possibilities, thousands of dollars are won by the kids. In avoiding biases such as the gambler's fallacy, the film demonstrates the outcomes of betting on the best statistical outcomes. Popular culture is more concerned with avoiding such biases as opposed to the research. *21* (Spacey and Luketic, 2008) view the gambler's fallacy and Bayes's Theorem as being exploited and used for the purpose of financial gain while research attempts to understand the bias and theorem for the purpose of uncovering the ways in which individuals can be swayed among differing lines of thought and judgment. Research differs from the popular fiction how it views this knowledge being used. Research examines biases such as the gambler's fallacy to attempt to predict how individuals will react. Popular fiction is more interested in exploiting how reality will play out as opposed to the person's behavior.

In examining the judgment making processes of individuals, several implications can be seen in the real world. Firstly, one can utilize biases to predict the behaviors of consumers when marketing products and examining trends and fads. Secondly, Bayes's Theorem can be used to assist individuals in realizing the flaws in their judgments and how they are persuaded by advertisements and media influence to make inaccurate decisions. Thirdly, Bayes's Theorem could be used to determine the likelihood of individuals utilizing such an understanding of human behavior for their own self-interest like how probabilities were used in *21* (Spacey and Luketic, 2008) for personal gain. In further examining the issue, the gambler's fallacy could be used to address whether an individual tends to be swayed more like toward a pessimistic belief or optimistic belief as opposed to sound logic. In using this applicable knowledge, an individual would have a better understanding of his or her own judgment and be able to adjust according so as to be better aware of when they are being unsuspectingly persuaded by other individuals, the media, or advertisements to make decisions that are less than the best possible decisions. In essence, an improved understanding of the biases that affect decisions making will allow individuals to be less susceptible to the exploitation of such biases.

Language of Ideas

The concept of language being used as a representation of mental concepts is directly related to the study of cognition and communication. Language serves as one of the primary methods for which individuals communicate ideas between each other. Without language, the abstract ideas and examples of concepts would be locked away in the mind of an individual and not be able to be conveyed to others. In examining the concept of language portraying ideas, numerous psychological are terms are relevant in understanding how this process works. Embodied cognition is a highly relevant term that has been used in numerous studies along with popular fiction references. Embodied cognition involves relating the processing of the mind to the physical structure of the body. The concept of semantics is also a highly relevant term when examining this topic since semantics refers to the meanings of sentences. Other areas of psychology as the study of social psychology, memory, and problem solving also have a great deal of interest in the concept of language being used as an expression of the mental constructions within an individual's mind.

In examining how individuals have utilized language to represent mental ideas, several studies have been conducted. Zwaan (2009) examined the theory of mental stimulation concerning language comprehension. In the study, several challenges arose against the concept of embodied cognition as an explanation of how the mind process the information presented to it from comprehending language. To challenge the idea of the mind responding similarly to language comprehension as it would motor activity, Zwaan (2009) examined responses to individual phonemes and words that would not have a response that could be easily represented by an embodied reaction from the individual. Rueschemeyer, Lindeman., Elk., and Bekkering (2009) examined the effects of words that were similar to a task that an individual was performing would affect the performance of the task if the words were processed by the individual while performing the task. The results revealed that the words similar to the task primed the individual in performing the task and improved response times to the tasks. A unique relationship existed in the research between the movements of objects towards and away from the body if the word was an object that would be associated with a similar movement that was either towards or away from the body. If the word was associated with the opposing movement in relationship to the body, response times would be less. The research of Rueschmeyer et al. (2009) displays an effect resonance between processing and motor processing that would be support of embodied cognition in relation to language. An interesting to pose concerning further research would be to examine if the performance of tasks while hearing the tasks in a classroom environment could improve learning of new information among individuals.

Popular fiction has taken a different approach when examining how language is used by individuals. In the film *Nell* (Foster & Apted, 1994), the topic viewed by examining a woman that had grown up being isolated from society. The woman developed her own language based on the necessity of communicating what things were. Since the woman was isolated from other people, the question arises concerning why she used the language and what function did it serve since she did not have others to communicate. *Nell* (Foster & Apted, 1994) clearly showed how the woman was did not react as one would expect to certain words as the words did not possess a meaning to her. In looking at the unique case, popular fiction creates some unique ideas about how language is used by individuals as representations of the external world and how that words invoke a lack of response once they have lost meaning.

In comparing popular fiction to research, one can note similarities between how research has noted that the meaning of a word primes an individual in performing tasks and how popular fiction addresses reactions of individuals to language based on meaning. The differences between the two concern the emphasis of how language is understood. In the research, language is examined to determine if responses can be generated by language in general regardless of meaning. Research has, however, revealed that the perceived meaning of language greatly influence how the language affects the performance and response of an individual. Popular fiction is more concerned with addressing how language develops in the absence of external influences to impact the individual in an isolated environment. The textbook provides several theories on language processing concerning its interpretation in the context of the complete information that it is presented and also concerning how it is structured regarding the manner in which external information is generally processed by the mind.

Further research into the perception of language could greatly advance science's understanding of how an individual understands the world. In understanding the manner in which individuals process language, learning materials could be better developed to improve how information is learned and process more effectively. In addition, studies could also provide leaders with improved skills that would allow for a better understanding and reduce miscommunications. Such implications could be far reaching into various facets of industry, education, and policies that impact countless people by providing a clear understanding of the presented expectations.

References

Foster, J. (Producer) & Apted, M.(Director). (1994). *Nell* [Motion Picture]. United States: Twentieth Century Fox Film Corporation

Rueschemeyer, S., Lindemann, O., Elk, M., & Bekkering, H. (2009). Embodied cognition: The interplay between automatic resonance and selection-for-action mechanisms. *European Journal Of Social Psychology*, *39*(7), 1180-1187. doi:10.1002/ejsp.662.

Zwaan, R. A. (2009). Mental simulation in language comprehension and social cognition. *European Journal Of Social Psychology*, *39*(7), 1142-1150. doi:10.1002/ejsp.661.

Johnson, J., Tellis, G., & Macinnis, D. (2005). Losers, Winners, and Biased

Trades. *Journal of Consumer Research*, *32*(2), 324-329.

Ross, B., & Degroot F. (1982). How Adolescences Combine Probabilities. *Journal of Psychology*, *110*(1), 75.

Spacey, K. [Producer] & Luketic, R. [Director]. 2008. *21* [Motion Picture]. United States: Columbia Pictures

Cameron, J. F. (Director & Producer), Austin, S. (Producer), Rack, B. J. (Producer), Hurd, G. A. (Producer), & Kassar, M. F. (Producer). (1991). *Terminator 2: Judgment Day* [Motion Picture]. United States: TriStar Pictures.

Cleophas, T. J., & Cleophas, T. F. (2010). Artificial intelligence for diagnostic purposes: principles, procedures and limitations. *Clinical Chemistry & Laboratory Medicine, 48*(2), 159-165. doi:10.1515/CCLM.2010.045.

Ptolemy, B. (Director & Producer), & Ptolemy F. (Producer). (2009). *Transcendent Man* [Motion Picture]. United States: Docurama

Shelley, M. W. (1994). *Frankenstein.* Retreived from http://etext.virginia.edu/toc/modeng/public/SheFran.html.

Chang, T. (Producer), Davis, J. (Producer), Hackett, M. (Producer), & Woo J. (Director). (2003). *Paycheck* [Motion Picture]. United States: DreamWorks Pictures.

Dewar, M., Della Sala, S., Beschin, N., & Cowan, N. (2010). Profound retroactive interference in

anterograde amnesia: What
interferes?. *Neuropsychology*, *24*(3),
357-367. doi:10.1037/a0018207

Diamond, R. J., & Rozin, P. (1984).
Activation of existing memories in
anterograde amnesia. *Journal of
Abnormal Psychology*, *93*(1), 98-
105. doi:10.1037/0021-843X.93.1.98